C IS FOR

CHRISTMAS

ALWAYS FOR MARK,
WHO ENCOURAGES ME.
AND FOR MY MOM AND DAD,
WHO LOVE ME NO MATTER WHAT!

Cover: *Light of Love* © Mark Missman. For print information, go to www.sagebrushfineart.com or call 801.466.5136

Page iv–1: *The Herald Angels* © 2012 Howard Lyon. For print information, go to www.fineart.howardlyon.com or call 480.241.7907

Page 2: *Cookies* © David McClellan. For more information, go to davemcclellan.blogspot.com

Page 3: *The Turkey* © 2012 Boston Madsen. For more information, go to www.bostonillustration.com

Page 4–5: *Christmas Wish* © Jean Monti, courtesy of The Greenwich Workshop, Inc. www.greenwichworkshop.com

Page 6: *Gifts* © 2012 Boston Madsen. For more information, go to www.bostonillustration.com

Page 7: *Light of Love* © Mark Missman. For print information, go to www.sagebrushfineart.com or call 801.466.5136

Pages 8–9: *A Christmas Eve Delivery* © William S. Phillips, courtesy of The Greenwich Workshop, Inc. www.greenwichworkshop.com

Page 10: *Christmas at Grandma's* Copyrights property of Sandra Kuck. For further information, contact jwkuck@msn,com.

Page 11: *Mistletoe* © 2012 Boston Madsen. For more information, go to www.bostonillustration.com

Pages 12–13: *Christmas Eve at the Winchester Inn* © William S. Phillips, courtesy of The Greenwich Workshop, Inc. www.greenwichworkshop.com

Pages 14–15: *Nativity* © Mark Missman. For print information, go to www.sagebrushfineart.com or call 801.466.5136

Page 16: *Christmas Memories* © Jean Monti, courtesy of The Greenwich Workshop, Inc. www.greenwichworkshop.com

Page 17: *Poinsettias* © 2012 Boston Madsen. For more information, go to www.bostonillustration.com

Pages 18–19: *Glad Tidings* © Joseph F. Brickey. For more information, go to www.josephbrickey.com

Page 20–21: *Visions of Sugar Plums* © 2012 Tom Browning. For more information, go to www.tombrowning.com

Pages 22–23: *Christmas Day* Copyrights property of Sandra Kuck. For further information, contact jwkuck@msn.com

Page 24: *Heaven's Perfect Gift* © Mark Missman. For print information, go to www.sagebrushfineart.com or call 801.466.5136

Page 25: *Wisemen Seek Him Still* © Mark Missman. For print information, go to www.sagebrushfineart.com or call 801.466.5136

Pages 26–27: *Asleep* © David McClellan. For more information, go to davemcclellan.blogspot.com

Page 28: *Falling* © Ben Sowards. For more information, go to www.bensowards.com

Cover design copyright © 2012 by Covenant Communications, Inc.
Jacket and book designed by Christina Marcano © 2012 Covenant Communications

Published by Covenant Communications, Inc.
American Fork, Utah

Copyright © 2012 by Tonya Skousen Arenaz

Printed in China
First Printing: October 2012

17 16 15 14   10 9 8 7 6 5 4

ISBN-13: 978-1-60861-365-6

C IS FOR CHRISTMAS

Tonya Skousen Arenaz

A is for Angels and
the Anthems they sing
announcing the birth of
our Savior and King.

B is for Bethlehem where
a Baby was Born
a long time ago
on the first Christmas morn.

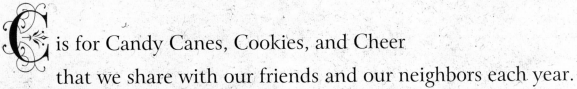

C is for Candy Canes, Cookies, and Cheer
that we share with our friends and our neighbors each year.

D is for Dinner, a table that's spread
with turkey and dressing and sweet Christmas bread.

E is for Eyes
that are Eager to see
all that is under
the Evergreen tree.

F is for Families
gathered together
for holiday Fun,
no matter the weather.

G is for Gratitude for Gifts we've been Given,
  the ones we unwrap and the ones straight from heaven.

H is for Happiness, the feeling we find
  as we think of the Christ child, the infant divine.

I is for Icicles, shiny and bright,
reflecting the glow of each Christmas tree light.

J is for Jingle bells and the carols we sing
and for all of the Joy that this holiday brings.

K is for Kisses beneath mistletoe
and for all of the Kindness that good people show.

L is for Lights
that glimmer above
on treetops and rooftops
reflecting Christ's Love.

M's for the Manger
where a new baby lay
all snuggly and warm on a
Mound of fresh hay.

N's for the Nativity
that seems New every year;
each small china figure
is precious and dear.

 is for Ornaments adorning each limb
and for Overstuffed stockings that are filled to the brim.

P is for Poinsettias, flowers so bold.
Their Perfect red color defies winter's cold.

Q is how Quickly the shepherds did go
To the small, Quiet stable in the town down below.

R is for Ribbons
and Rudolph's Red nose
and Reindeer that frolic
through cold winter snows.

S is for Santa,
who comes while we sleep.
He leaves us Surprises
and treasures to keep.

T is for *Tannenbaum*,
a word for the Tree.
With Trimmings
and Tinsel, it's pretty to see.

U's for the gift
that's not Under a tree—
the Undying love
that Christ gives you and me.

 is for Mary, the Virgin so mild,
a Virtuous mother for this special child.

W is for Wise Men who Wandered afar
and Watched for a baby born under a star.

X is for the eXcitement
we eXpress with our laughter
and all the eXhaustion
we feel the day after.

Y is for the Yule log
burning Yellow and red,
keeping You warm
'til You crawl into bed.

$\mathbb{Z}$ is for ZZZZZs as we sleep in our beds,
while holiday memories dance in our heads.